Role and Direction of Nuclear Regulatory Research

Summary of Expert Panel Report

U.S. Nuclear Regulatory Commission
Office of Nuclear Regulatory Research
Washington, DC 20555-0001

AVAILABILITY OF REFERENCE MATERIALS
IN NRC PUBLICATIONS

NRC Reference Material

As of November 1999, you may electronically access NUREG-series publications and other NRC records at NRC's Public Electronic Reading Room at www.nrc.gov/NRC/ADAMS/index.html.
Publicly released records include, to name a few, NUREG-series publications; *Federal Register* notices; applicant, licensee, and vendor documents and correspondence; NRC correspondence and internal memoranda; bulletins and information notices; inspection and investigative reports; licensee event reports; and Commission papers and their attachments.

NRC publications in the NUREG series, NRC regulations, and *Title 10, Energy*, in the Code of *Federal Regulations* may also be purchased from one of these two sources.
1. The Superintendent of Documents
   U.S. Government Printing Office
   Mail Stop SSOP
   Washington, DC 20402–0001
   Internet: bookstore.gpo.gov
   Telephone: 202-512-1800
   Fax: 202-512-2250
2. The National Technical Information Service
   Springfield, VA 22161–0002
   www.ntis.gov
   1–800–553–6847 or, locally, 703–605–6000

A single copy of each NRC draft report for comment is available free, to the extent of supply, upon written request as follows:
Address: Office of the Chief Information Officer,
           Reproduction and Distribution
             Services Section
           U.S. Nuclear Regulatory Commission
           Washington, DC 20555-0001
E-mail: DISTRIBUTION@nrc.gov
Facsimile: 301–415–2289

Some publications in the NUREG series that are posted at NRC's Web site address www.nrc.gov/NRC/NUREGS/indexnum.html are updated periodically and may differ from the last printed version. Although references to material found on a Web site bear the date the material was accessed, the material available on the date cited may subsequently be removed from the site.

Non-NRC Reference Material

Documents available from public and special technical libraries include all open literature items, such as books, journal articles, and transactions, *Federal Register* notices, Federal and State legislation, and congressional reports. Such documents as theses, dissertations, foreign reports and translations, and non-NRC conference proceedings may be purchased from their sponsoring organization.

Copies of industry codes and standards used in a substantive manner in the NRC regulatory process are maintained at—
       The NRC Technical Library
       Two White Flint North
       11545 Rockville Pike
       Rockville, MD 20852–2738

These standards are available in the library for reference use by the public. Codes and standards are usually copyrighted and may be purchased from the originating organization or, if they are American National Standards, from—
       American National Standards Institute
       11 West 42nd Street
       New York, NY 10036–8002
       www.ansi.org
       212–642–4900

NUREG-1802, Vol. 1

Role and Direction of Nuclear Regulatory Research

Summary of Expert Panel Report

Manuscript Completed: September 2001
Date Published: September 2001

Prepared by
R. W. Durante, Durante Associates

Under Contract to
Arthur Andersen, LLP
1150 17th Street, NW
Washington, DC 20036-4613

and

J.W. Johnson, U.S. Nuclear Regulatory Commission

Office of Nuclear Regulatory Research
U.S. Nuclear Regulatory Commission
Washington, DC 20555-0001

Abstract

This report summarizes the input received from a 17-member Panel of Experts on the role and future direction of nuclear regulatory research. Membership on the panel was comprised of representatives from Congress, government, industry, universities, private consultants, international, and the public. Major focus areas of discussions included research funding, cooperative research, infrastructure, and communication. The work of the panel was divided into two phases. Phase 1 focused on the vision, mission, and general direction of regulatory research. Phase II provided guidance and perspectives on the future direction of regulatory research.

TABLE OF CONTENTS

Acknowledgments

In 1974, Congress mandated the formation of the Office of Nuclear Regulatory Research to ensure "an independent capability for developing and analyzing technical information related to reactor safety, safeguards and environmental protection in support of the licensing and regulatory process." The Nuclear Regulatory Commission's regulatory research program continues to provide a significant part of the Commission's independent technical capability. The scope and emphasis of NRC's reactor research program have changed over the years as nuclear technology has changed and continues to evolve. As a means of supplementing our internal planning, it is essential that we seek stakeholder input on the role and future direction of regulatory research. To accomplish this goal an Expert Panel was formed consisting of representatives from Congress, government, industry, universities, private consultants, international, and the public. The panel was chaired by Dr. Kenneth C. Rogers. Mr. Raymond W. Durante served as the panel coordinator.

The work of the panel was divided into two phases. Phase 1 focused on the vision, mission, and general direction of regulatory research. Phase II provided guidance and perspectives on the future direction of regulatory research. The Members of the Expert Panel volunteered their time and resources to support this important agency initiative. The Commission was briefed by representatives of the Expert Panel on May 10, 2001 on their findings. The Commission expressed their appreciation to the Panel and commended them for a job well done. I also wish to express my appreciation to the panel for their invaluable contributions on topics of immense value to the NRC as we plan the role of regulatory research in a rapidly changing environment in the nuclear industry and the regulatory arena.

Ashok C. Thadani, Director
Office of Nuclear Regulatory Research
U.S. Nuclear Regulatory Commission

INTRODUCTION

The Nuclear Industry is currently involved in important and far-reaching changes that are creating new issues and new challenges for the Nuclear Regulatory Commission (NRC). As a result, the Agency is currently involved in an internal evaluation to determine how it can meet these challenges and at the same time continue its objectives to maintain safety; protect the environment and the common defense and security; increase public confidence; make NRC activities and decisions more effective, efficient, and realistic; and reduce unnecessary regulatory burdens on stakeholders. An essential part of this effort is a thorough review of the activities of the Office of Nuclear Regulatory Research (RES). Since it was established by Congress in 1975, RES has provided a significant part of NRC's independent capability for developing and analyzing technical information related to reactor safety, safeguards, and environmental protection in support of the licensing and regulatory process.

As a means of supplementing internal planning, input from stakeholders was sought on the role and future direction of RES in this rapidly changing environment. A 17-member panel of experts (chaired by former Commissioner Kenneth Rogers and representing industry, academia, government, and public interest groups) was assembled and asked to present their views and comments on the vision, mission, role, and general direction of regulatory research and to provide insight and guidance for future activities. A list of the members, all of whom who served voluntarily, is included in Volume I of this report.

The work on this report was divided into two phases and the Panel was convened for two meetings for each phase. The first two-day meeting was opened by NRC Chairman Richard Meserve, followed by presentations from and open discussions with senior RES staff. The panel met the next day for internal discussions and then adjourned. Individual preliminary written statements were submitted by each of the members identifying key issues and recommendations. The second meeting involved only the panel and focused on more detailed discussions of individual statements, which were then finalized by the authors and included as part of this report. The objective of Phase 1 was to broadly examine the mission and role of RES and its contribution to the basic objectives of the NRC. Since this was a non-FACA panel (Federal Advisory Committee Act), no attempt was made to develop a consensus report; instead, members were encouraged to present their own individual viewpoints and recommendations. However, based on the information from the written submissions and discussions during the meetings, there appeared to be several conclusions and recommendations widely shared by many panel members. These issues were restated in the form of recommendations to the Commission, and for the Phase 2 effort, the Panel was asked for their individual suggestions and comments as to how these recommendations could be implemented. Phase 2 was conducted in a similar manner with a two-day and a one-day meeting in which presentations were made to the panel by NRR, NMSS, RES, and representatives of the regions. Prior to the meetings, the panel requested and was provided with detailed information on budgets, programs, and specific activities of these offices.

The panel submitted their individual comments and recommendations that are included in Volume II. At the onset of Phase 1, in his opening address to the Panel, Chairman Meserve offered three questions for the panel's consideration. There were preliminary responses to theses questions in Phase 1; however, the panel requested and was provided with more information in order to provide more substantive answers. The three questions and the individual final responses are included in Volume II of this report.

It should be strongly emphasized that this panel was a non-FACA committee and there was no attempt to reach a consensus. The material in this report represents the unique viewpoints of the panel members based on their experience and understanding of research as it is conducted by the NRC. The views of the panel members, including the Chairman, are their own with no editing or modification; they are included in their entirety in Volume II. Volume I is a summary, written by a non-member of the panel, that summarizes the positions commonly held by a majority of the panel members, including conclusions and recommendations which appeared to be most widely shared.

UNITED STATES
NUCLEAR REGULATORY COMMISSION
WASHINGTON, D.C. 20555-0001
July 3, 2000

Dr. Kenneth Rogers
6202 Perthshire Court
Bethesda, MD 20817

Dear Dr. Rogers:

The Nuclear Regulatory Commission is currently involved in a number of important changes we believe will improve safety, regulatory efficiency, and improve public confidence. An essential ingredient for success in these new initiatives is a sound research program. Since it was established by Congressional action in 1975, the Office of Nuclear Regulatory Research has provided a significant part of the Commission's independent capability and will most assuredly continue to be an important resource in the future.

As a means of supplementing our internal planning, we are seeking input from stakeholders on the future direction of regulatory research. The approach we are taking is to obtain the views of experts from government, industry, and the public to meet with research staff and provide insight and guidance for future research programs. This effort would be undertaken in two phases. Phase I would focus on the vision, mission, and general direction of regulatory research. Phase II would provide specific guidance and perspectives on the future direction of regulatory research.

I am writing to you to invite you to participate as an expert for Phase I. The membership for Phase II will be determined at a later date. Your contributions along with those of other experts who have been carefully chosen will help NRC plan the role of its research in what is clearly a rapidly changing environment in the nuclear industry and regulatory arena. The resulting input will help ensure NRC's decisions have a strong technical base, are clearly understood by the public and the regulated industry, and provide the NRC with the tools to anticipate and proactively address this ever changing environment.

The first meeting will be held in the Washington, DC, area on August 16-17. Specific details, including a list of other experts, are enclosed.

For additional information, please contact Mr. Ashok C. Thadani, Director of the Office of Nuclear Regulatory Research. Mr. Thadani's mailing address, telephone number, and e-mail address are:

> Ashok C. Thadani, Director
> Office of Nuclear Regulatory Research
> U.S. Nuclear Regulatory Commission
> Washington, DC 20555-0001
> (301) 415-6641
> E-mail: ACT@ NRC.GOV

Dr. Kenneth Rogers

If you need assistance with your travel arrangements and hotel accommodations, please contact Mr. James W. Johnson of Mr. Thadani's staff. Mr. Johnson can be reached on (301) 415-6293.

1 look forward to your participation and help in charting an appropriate course for NRC's research activities.

Sincerely,

William D. Travers
Executive Director
for Operations

Enclosures: As stated

EXPERT PANEL MEMBERS

Panel Chairman: Dr. Kenneth C. Rogers Former NRC Commissioner	Panel Coordinator: Raymond W. Durante Arthur Andersen
Dr. John F. Ahearne Director Sigma XI Research Triangle Park, NC	Dr. Theodore U. Marston VP and Chief Nuclear Officer Electric Power Research Institute Palo Alto, CA
Dr. Robert J. Budnitz President Future Resources Associates, Inc. Berkeley, CA	Dr. Dominic J. Monetta Resource Alternatives, Inc. Washington, DC
Mr. David R. Helwig Commonwealth Edison Downers Grove, IL	Dr. Kenneth L. Mossman Director, Office of Radiation Safety Arizona State University Tempe, AR
Dr. Michel Livolant* Director Institute de Protection et ed Surete Nucleaire (IPSN) Cedex, France	Dr. Thomas E. Murley Consultant Bethesda, MD
Dr. David Lochbaum* Nuclear Safety Engineer Union of Concerned Scientists Washington, DC	Mr. Harold B. Ray Executive VP Southern California Edison Rosemead, CA
Dr. Jane C.S. Long Dean, Mackay School of Mines University of Nevada, Reno	Kristine L. Svinicki Legislative Fellow (Senator Craig) Washington, DC
Dr. Edwin Lyman Nuclear Control Institute Washington, DC	J. Aloysius Hogan Counsel (Senator Hagel) Washington, DC
Dr. William D. Magwood, IV Director, Nuclear Energy, Science and Technology U.S. Department of Energy Washington, DC	Andrew R. Wheeler* Counsel, Senate Committee on Environment and Public Works Washington, DC
Mr. Alexander Marion Nuclear Energy Institute Washington, DC	
Alternates	
Dr. William H. Bohlke Exelon Generation Downers Grove, IL	Dr. Paul Leventhal Nuclear Control Institute Washington, DC
Dr. John Gaertner EPRI Charlotte, NC	A. Edward Scherer Southern California Edison San Clemente, CA

* Participated in Phase I only.

SUMMARY

PHASE I

The 17 statements presented in this report are the views of individual panel members, including the Chairman. No attempt has been made to reach a consensus or establish a uniform set of recommendations. It is clear, however, many issues and conclusions were independently considered by more than one panel member, and in some cases a majority of the panel. The submissions of the individual panelists contain many unique and important comments and ideas that merit serious consideration; therefore, all the individual statements should be reviewed in addition to this summary. Issues considered most prevalent are discussed below.

The panel members were in general agreement that a strong viable RES with world class expertise must be maintained in order to ensure a sound technical base for all NRC activities and to maintain the credibility and leadership role of the NRC both domestically and internationally. Most panel members were of the opinion that RES must expand in-house expertise by adding experienced professionals, qualified in areas directly related to current and anticipated regulatory activities. There was no criticism of current personnel, but it was felt that, through attrition and budget reductions, technical expertise has been steadily eroded in some technical areas. It was suggested that RES have a cadre of full time in-house technical experts available to keep abreast of worldwide technical developments that might impact on regulatory activities.

There was general concern that the physical facilities available to RES are showing their age and rapidly becoming obsolete and expensive to operate, particularly those of the National Laboratories. Many of these facilities, as well as those at universities and in private industry, are being shut down prematurely for economic reasons. NRC must work with industry and other government agencies to make a case for maintaining these facilities in preparation for future work. There was concern that, in order to maintain independence, RES was forced to utilize government facilities that were obsolete or inadequate. This prompted further discussion by several members of the panel on the need for more collaborative efforts, using the resources and facilities of industry and international sources. Successful collaborative efforts in the past with foreign-owned facilities were cited as examples.

There were extensive discussions regarding the question of whether the NRC can maintain independence in its decision making while utilizing data and test results obtained by others. It was generally agreed that a solution to this dilemma must be found, and most of the panel members commented on this topic. Most of the panel members recommended RES increase its cooperative research efforts with DOE, industry, EPRI, and international organizations. It was felt that, with declining budgets, pooling research efforts with others would result in more effective use of available resources and this practice should be more frequently utilized. It was suggested that RES would not necessarily have to initiate or manage all research efforts, but it must be in on the planning and establishing of objectives for such research programs that it needs to use. It was recommended that current working agreements with DOE and

EPRI be re-examined and strengthened wherever possible and more fully utilized. There was concern, however, that RES not rely solely on the advice and guidance of those organizations that might ultimately do the research.

An underlying concern among several panel members was whether RES was operating in accordance with the intent of the original congressional mandate. The question was raised as to whether all research should be conducted in a single organization, i.e., RES. Members differed on this issue; however, several felt that a single strong center conducting all research for the Agency should be considered. There was considerable discussion regarding the proper balance between anticipatory and confirmatory research and technical support, with general agreement among the members that the current mix of anticipatory and confirmatory research appears to be reasonable. There were questions on how decisions are made, what anticipatory research is done, and what objectives are sought. Several members of the panel stated that costs for anticipatory research should not be recovered through fees, but from general funds. Several panel members suggested the definition of research as it is conducted by the NRC should be more clearly defined, and more transparent methods are needed to decide what research needs to be done and when to start and when to terminate research projects.

The crosscutting issue that impacted all other issues was funding the RES efforts. It was generally agreed that funding was at a dangerously low level and any further cuts would make the viability of RES questionable. The need for full cost recovery places too much burden on stakeholders, and opinions ranged from funding RES completely from general funds to at least providing a significant percentage from that source. Several panel members felt stakeholders should not be required to fund any anticipatory research, even though such research has value and may be needed for future regulatory actions. It was suggested that the NRC at the highest levels increase contact and dialogue with the Congress to obtain budget relief and reconsideration of the requirement for full cost recovery. Support by the nuclear industry in this effort was regarded as essential for its success.

A majority of the panel agreed that RES must improve its communications efforts with the stakeholders, other government agencies, and internally with the Commission at all organizational levels. Concern was expressed that in many instances the public and even industry are unaware of what RES programs were under way, the objectives being pursued, the final results, and how these results were used for regulatory purposes.

Several panel members urged more active and direct leadership by the Commissioners in support of RES both internally and externally to underscore the value of the research performed at the NRC in support of nuclear safety domestically and worldwide. Support from stakeholders, particularly the industry and DOE, is needed to achieve this objective.

Finally, it should be noted that at the first panel meeting NRC Chairman Meserve, in his opening remarks, posed three questions to the panel and most of the members attempted to respond directly to these questions. These individual responses are included in Volume II.

PHASE II

The objectives of Phase 2 of the expert panel were to identify key policy recommendations to the Commission that were developed in Phase 1 and suggest ways and means to implement these recommendations. There was general agreement on the importance of maintaining and supporting a strong research capability to ensure the safety of U.S. nuclear facilities and contribute to U.S. leadership in nuclear technology worldwide; therefore, the panel focused on identifying strategies to achieve this objective. While there was no attempt to establish a consensus among the panel members, similar specific recommendations were made by a significant number of panel members, in some cases the majority, for actions to be taken by the Commissioners, EDO, and RES to improve and enhance RES operations. The scope of attention given by the panel members was extremely broad and covered a wide range of RES operations and interrelationships with the other program offices. In order to produce a manageable analysis, the individual panel members' comments and recommendations that appeared most often were combined into four major policy-type recommendations. The panel was asked to focus on these recommendations and present their views and suggestions as to how they might be implemented. The four recommendations are listed below, followed by brief statements on how they might be implemented. It should be emphasized that since this is a summary only the suggestions that appeared most often are included. There are other important issues and recommendations made by individual panel members that should be considered. For this reason it is important to review the individual statements of each panel member as contained in Volume II of this report.

Specific Recommendations

1. The NRC must maintain, as a used and useful arm of its organization, a reliable, respected Office of Nuclear Regulatory Research and must support this office with the necessary people and resources so it is an unassailable source of technical information and support for regulatory actions. This is necessary not only to establish the credibility of NRC's technical decision making and thereby ensure the safety of all NRC licensed activities, but also to ensure U.S. leadership in the technology of nuclear safety regulation.

   a. RES was established by legislation and given a mandate to ensure an independent capability for developing and analyzing technical information related to reactor safety, safeguards, and environmental protection in support of the licensing and regulatory process. The Commission should explore ways to increase the funding for RES in order for this responsibility to be adequately carried out.

   b. The Commission should direct the EDO to establish minimum requirements for RES core capabilities and resources required for maintaining the necessary people, analytical tools, and access to facilities.

c.   The Commission should charge RES with monitoring the Agency's state of readiness to meet future challenges as a result of new technologies, advances in reactor design, safety issues, and industry initiatives and to report its findings to the Commission on a periodic basis (e.g., biennially).

2.   RES must support the activities of other program offices, which in turn should be required to coordinate their activities with RES at least to the extent of planning new work, establishing objectives of technical studies, and assessing the validity of data and analyses. At the same time, RES should be allowed to initiate anticipatory technical studies without approval by program offices, but with their cognizance and input wherever possible. RES must be able to do and be seen as able to do independent verification of data that NRC will rely on for regulatory action. RES must institute and maintain a comprehensive and effective communications program to make available its plans and activities.

a.   The Commission should require RES to develop a strategic oversight system for its anticipatory research and require input from the program offices in both identifying and prioritizing anticipatory work. However, the decisions on an anticipatory research program must lie with the Director of the Office of Nuclear Regulatory Research. RES should provide the Commission with annual reports on the results of its anticipatory research program.

b.   The Commission should encourage the expansion of RES activities beyond narrow technical activities and task RES with responsibility for identifying new systems-wide issues that could have significant safety implications and for proposing further relevant studies. Examples might be the impact of regulation on a licensee's safety culture and the positive or negative synergistic results of current or new regulations or new industry initiatives.

c.   The Commission should direct RES to improve communications with stakeholders on its research program. RES programs should be described in understandable language in reports including, but not limited to, an annual RES report that describes the purpose of the research, the expected use in the regulatory process, and sunset criteria for each major research program.

3.   RES must continue to increase its cooperative efforts with other organizations including, but not necessarily limited to, EPRI, DOE, industry, academia, public interest groups, and international organizations. RES must seek out and, wherever possible, utilize facilities, equipment, and resources available from these entities and maximize the use of technical data and results already developed. RES, in cooperation with and supported by the Commission, must establish procedures to accomplish this while fully retaining the decision making independence of RES.

a.   The Commission should direct RES to expand its base of contractors to include more private organizations. RES should explore innovative ways to contract with private organizations that will not significantly delay the contracting process.

b.   The Commission should direct RES to identify inhibitors to further expansion of cooperative research with the international community, EPRI, DOE, and the nuclear industry and to propose for Commission consideration strategies to implement such cooperative research without compromising NRC's independent regulatory decision making.

4.   A clear and understandable definition of what research includes and does not include at the NRC and its value to the safety of the nation's nuclear program must be established by the Commission and accepted internally by the program offices and staff personnel and effectively conveyed to all the stakeholders. Continuing efforts must be made through research to eliminate unnecessary regulatory burdens on stakeholders while at the same time focusing on areas that will benefit them through safer and more efficient operations. Charges to licensees for research costs should be on the basis of identifiable value to the efficient and effective regulation of those licensees.

a.   The Commission should establish a clear concise definition of research as it is conducted by this agency, with clear distinction among anticipatory research, confirmatory research, and technical assistance and the significance of "realistic" in a RES context.

b.   The Commission should support adjustments to the fee structure to ensure that funding derived from licensee fees is used only to support the regulatory needs of those licensees. Funding for new technology and advanced designs should be independent of the fee structure.

In addition to the four policy recommendations given above, the panel was also asked to respond to three questions posed by Chairman Meserve at the opening meeting. These questions are listed below with brief responses, representative of the most commonly held positions of the individual panel members. It should be stressed again that for the sake of brevity only the most often expressed comments were summarized. There are other important comments included in the individual statements by each of the panel members and these statements should be carefully reviewed.

RESPONSES TO THE CHAIRMAN'S THREE QUESTIONS

At the onset of Phase 1, the Chairman emphasized the importance of this study to assist the Commission in chartering future tasks of the RES. Chairman Meserve stated that, among other things, he was seeking answers to the following questions:

1.   Are we spending enough on research?
2.   Are we doing the right research?
3.   Are we doing research with the right people?

While most panel members provided opinions on these questions, all members indicated they did not have enough material or background information to properly address these questions. As a result, Phase 2 presentations were made by NRR and NMSS describing research activities relative to user needs and RES described the anticipatory research being done. Based on this more detailed information, the panel was able to provide more specific answers to the questions. It should be emphasized that in Phase 2, which was conducted in the same manner as Phase 1 as a non-FACA committee and a non-consensus report, there were a number of comments and recommendations by more than one member of the panel and in cases a majority of the panel. The comments and recommendations below represent a combination of Phases 1 and 2 material submitted by the expert panel.

1.   <u>Are We Spending Enough on Research</u>?   Based on the presentation by RES, it was concluded that research in general and anticipatory research specifically are substantially under-funded. While not everyone provided numerical assessments, those who did put this shortfall in the range of $4-12 million per year. It was pointed out the research budget has been significantly reduced over the past 10 years while the challenges to research based on emerging issues have increased. It was stated that somewhere between 80-90 percent of the RES research budget is dedicated to user-need research. The remaining 10-20 percent did not appear to be adequate for RES to undertake research on emerging issues arising from decommissioning, license transfer, advanced technologies, license renewal, and other such activities. Several panel members felt RES should be able to challenge technical results from both NRR and NMSS technical support activities to be certain a sound technology database is being used in license decision making. A number of panel members expressed concern that RES's budget was insufficient to maintain its technical core capabilities needed in the face of declining staff throughout the Agency. It was suggested that RES increase its technical capability and expand its contractor services as well as the facilities that are used. This would require additional funding.

2.   <u>Are We Doing the Right Research</u>? The majority of panel members strongly indicated that not enough anticipatory research is being done and RES is not doing enough work in the material and waste areas. It was also suggested that RES should be doing more work on the utilization of PRA results and developing improved PRA methods, and RES should be working on improving data that

would permit the Commission to assume its goal of reducing the financial burden on stakeholders. Several panel members felt that, regardless of the work being done by NMSS in evaluating the ability to license waste management programs, special research skills are required to review that work and verify its credibility. Decisions regarding the ultimate safety of the Yucca Mountain Project, for example, will be carefully scrutinized by stakeholders and solid research data must be available to support the decisions made by the Commission. It was felt that by placing such a strong emphasis on research applied to user needs, significant gaps in technology will result that cannot be filled because of lack of funding and personnel. Although several panel members did not feel licensees should pay for anticipatory research, they recognized the need to perform this research. It was recommended that a more robust funding of research be pursued by the Commission with a larger percentage of the funding derived from the general funds appropriated by Congress instead of licensee fees. It was also recommended that a systematic process of prioritizing research projects be established with greater coordination between NRR and NMSS. Some panel members suggested that more communications with licensees and other stakeholders outside of NRC would increase the likelihood that the necessary research is being performed.

3. <u>Are We Doing Research with the Right People</u>? Several panel members pointed out that it was the intent of Congress for NRC to use DOE's national labs to take advantage of the large DOE budget for research. However, with a reduced RES budget, it becomes more difficult to conduct research with varied contractor types and at the same time sustain some minimum funding level to ensure quality products. The Commission must continue to find ways to use DOE laboratories as well as DOE resources. This can be done through collaborative efforts suggested by the NRC but carried out by the DOE. It was pointed out that complex contracting procedures can take too long to contract with organizations other than the national labs, and NRC should find ways to reduce the time it takes to contract with industry, academia, and other private organizations. It was stressed that this must be done carefully so the NRC in general and RES specifically do not diminish their independent roles or relinquish safety objectives in any way. Several panel members felt that anticipatory research, particularly long-term projects, can benefit by contributions from university teams that fit less-structured and less time-disciplined modes of operation. However, RES must continue to develop its skills in managing university research projects. RES should also review the working arrangements they currently have with EPRI and DOE to be certain they provide sufficient flexibility to maximize the benefits of the work being done by those two agencies without losing independent verification capabilities. It was also pointed out that advice on research provided to the NRC by the ACRS and the ACNW is excellent, but both of these committees are heavily burdened and some new mechanism could be created to provide additional oversight in the form of periodic reviews of NRC's overall research programs by a broad-based group of experts every two or three years. Specifically, it was recommended that the Commission require RES to review all its programs and reassess the unfunded-but-needed efforts and develop a set of required competencies and amount of funding required to perform these projects.

PANEL CHAIRMAN'S OPENING REMARKS

Expectations/Plans/Mode of Operation

Panel Chairman: Kenneth C. Rogers
August 16, 2000

Once again, welcome to you all who have generously agreed to contribute your time and thoughts to this NRC effort to ensure that its research activities are as valuable as possible in supporting the agency's responsibilities with regard to public health and safety and the environment. With your indulgence, I will call to mind some of the history behind our being here today.

The Energy Reorganization Act of 1974 replaced the Atomic Energy Commission by two new entities: The Energy Research and Development Administration and the Nuclear Regulatory Commission. The AEC was a very large, powerful and heavily funded agency with activities in all areas of nuclear technology, including promotion and development of the uses of nuclear materials as well as the regulation of their safe use. These functions were divided between the two new agencies with safety regulation of civilian uses assigned to the NRC and military uses and development and promotional activities for civilian uses assigned to ERDA. Both new agencies were supported by appropriations derived from general funds rather than from licensee fees, an important difference for NRC today.

The Act directed the establishment of the Office of Nuclear Regulatory Research with a Director reporting to the Commission and charged with

> **Developing recommendations** for research deemed necessary for performance of the Commission of its licensing and related regulatory functions
>
> **Engaging in** or **contracting for** research which the Commission deems necessary for the performance of its licensing and regulatory functions.

The NRC was not given any substantial laboratories of its own, but other federal agencies were expected to meet those needs of the NRC that require access to physical laboratories.

The Act further stated   "... **the head of every other federal agency shall**

> **cooperate** with respect to the establishment of priorities for the furnishing of such research services as requested by the Commission....
>
> **furnish** to the Commission, on a reimbursable basis, through their own facilities or by contract or other arrangement, such services as the Commission deems necessary....

consult and cooperate with the Commission on research and development matters of mutual interest and provide such information and physical access to its facilities as will assist the Commission in acquiring the expertise necessary to perform its licensing and related regulatory functions.

Clearly the Congress expected the NRC to have access to all federal facilities to obtain research information and to be billed for these services. It left up to the Commission to decide what kinds of research it would need and how and where it would acquire them.

Over the nearly 30 years that have passed since the NRC and the Office of Nuclear Regulatory Research were created, there have been vast changes in NRC's needs for information derived through the Office of Research and how meeting those needs is funded. The role of NRC research in the scientific and technological community world-wide has evolved, and a number of NRC-sponsored studies have had great impacts on the entire nuclear technology community and have resulted in NRC becoming regarded as a leading world-class authority.

Various reviews of NRC's research programs have been carried out. The most comprehensive study was conducted under the auspices of the National Research Council in 1986. Two of our own panel members were associated with that study, John Ahearne and Robert Budnitz. That study made a number of recommendations, and although the context in which they were made has changed considerably, many of its recommendations have relevance to today's world. In my view two of the study's most far reaching statements were the call for **routine use of peer review to instill confidence in the quality of research results**, and **establishment of a strong advisory group that includes independent experts from industry and academia along with representatives of organizations performing research.**

The NRC has been striving to strengthen all of its activities, and in my opinion, the convening of this panel is testimony to NRC's genuine effort towards continual self-improvement. I believe that the establishment of this panel is neither an exercise in self-justification by the NRC nor is it a response to an immediate acute problem. Rather, I view it as NRC's search for constructive criticisms from each and all of you as knowledgeable stakeholders. I see my role as Chairman as facilitating their development through a process involving **presentations** by NRC staff with ample opportunities for you to raise questions and to seek clarifications **and the sharing** of your own thoughts with your fellow panelists. I do ask you to forego taking issue with the NRC staff on any of the matters in their presentations and to reserve expression of those thoughts for **your** individual presentations to the panel on Thursday. Today should be directed towards probing, discovery, and clarification with analysis and recommendations for reinforcement or remediation put off until tomorrow. I will be amenable to accepting recommendations for improvements in today's process after it has had a chance to evolve during the day.

Before we turn to the presentations does anyone have a question or comment?

Mr. Thadani, Director of the Office of Nuclear Regulatory Research, will lead off.

Panel Chairman: Kenneth C. Rogers
February 21, 2001

NRC Experts Panel on Research

Welcome and thank you to everyone participating in our final panel meeting here or on line. Dr. Jane Long and Dr. Kenneth Mossman are with us via telephone.

This meeting is open to the public and we have with us some additional interested people seated around the room. Would you please introduce yourselves?

Welcome to you also.

We have two activities to complete today. The first is to share our individual comments on each of the four statements proposed for Commission consideration and action, and the second to have one last go around on our individual answers to Chairman Meserve's three questions to the panel and any related matters.

Following Mr. Thadani's comments on the work of the panel to date, I propose to take up our first task and complete it by 12:30 at which time we will break for lunch. We will resume our work at 1:30 by taking up the Chairman's questions and related matters with an objective of closing the meeting by 4:30.

Our time will be very tight, but if each of us tries to keep our comments to 5 minutes, I think that we all will have an opportunity to participate. I propose to take up the statements one at a time with suggestions for any truly significant wording changes in that policy statement and whatever suggestions you have for Commission actions to effectuate the policy. (Your final written submissions will provide the opportunity for fine scale wordsmithing.) Mr. Durante will put the essence of each comment on a poster sheet so we can all see how they stack up. These will be important for his summary and for my presentation to the Commission at a Commission meeting in May. I will invite your comments as in the past by going around the table.

But before we begin, Mr. Durante has some housekeeping information for us. Ray...

Thanks very much.

NRC FORM 335
(2-89)
NRCM 1102,
3201, 3202

U.S. NUCLEAR REGULATORY COMMISSION

BIBLIOGRAPHIC DATA SHEET

(See instructions on the reverse)

1. REPORT NUMBER
(Assigned by NRC, Add Vol., Supp., Rev., and Addendum Numbers, if any.)

NUREG-1802, Vol. 1

2. TITLE AND SUBTITLE

Role and Direction of Nuclear Regulatory Research

Summary of Expert Panel Report

3. DATE REPORT PUBLISHED

MONTH	YEAR
September	2001

4. FIN OR GRANT NUMBER

5. AUTHOR(S)

R.W. Durante, Durante Associates, under contract to Arthur Andersen, LLP
J.W. Johnson, NRC

6. TYPE OF REPORT

Technical

7. PERIOD COVERED *(Inclusive Dates)*

8. PERFORMING ORGANIZATION - NAME AND ADDRESS *(If NRC, provide Division, Office or Region, U.S. Nuclear Regulatory Commission, and mailing address; if contractor, provide name and mailing address.)*

Office of Nuclear Regulatory Research
U.S. Nuclear Regulatory Commission
Washington, DC 20555-0001

9. SPONSORING ORGANIZATION - NAME AND ADDRESS *(If NRC, type "Same as above"; if contractor, provide NRC Division, Office or Region, U.S. Nuclear Regulatory Commission, and mailing address.)*

Same as 8. above.

10. SUPPLEMENTARY NOTES

11. ABSTRACT *(200 words or less)*

This report summarizes the input received from a 17-member Panel of Experts on the role and future direction of nuclear regulatory research. Membership on the panel was comprised of representatives from Congress, government, industry, universities, private consultants, international, and the public. Major focus areas of discussion included research funding, cooperative research, infrastructure, and communication. The work of the panel was divided into two phases. Phase 1 focused on the vision, mission, and general direction of regulatory research. Phase 2 provided guidance and perspectives on the future direction of regulatory research.

12. KEY WORDS/DESCRIPTORS *(List words or phrases that will assist researchers in locating the report.)*

Regulatory research, confirmatory research, anticipatory research, cooperative research, infrastructure, communication, independence.

13. AVAILABILITY STATEMENT

unlimited

14. SECURITY CLASSIFICATION

(This Page)

unclassified

(This Report)

unclassified

15. NUMBER OF PAGES

16. PRICE

NRC FORM 335 (2-89)

This form was electronically produced by Elite Federal Forms, Inc.

Federal Recycling Program